TULPA

Louise Bak

COACH HOUSE BOOKS

FIRST EDITION

Published with the assistance of the Canada Council for the Arts and the Ontario Arts Council.

NATIONAL LIBRARY OF CANADA CATALOGUING IN PUBLICATION DATA

Bak, Louise, 1972–
Tulpa

Poems.
ISBN 1-55245-083-X

I. Title.

PS8553.A3696T85 2001 C811'.54 C2001-901838-X
PR9199.3.B34T85 2001

For my father, Edward Bak

Contents

Listening

Silent and lotus-postured under the maple tree,
Buddha's *bodhi* sprouting in my body.
Three branches dip like the triskelion,
rising and setting to the rhythm of the Serpent
that slides between the descant of the whales,
the tympani of the gorillas and the low whispers
of human voices, engrained in every truncheoned
annular ring and pericoloured torn-leaf tangram.

Mongolian *khummii* meditators call from the
cardboard box thrown into the crusher by two garbage
collectors across the street. The grumbling truck's
jowls close on another pile of fish fin in
Chinatown's Great Wall of refuse, rebuilt every day
by grocers, peel spitters and solitary women
who mutter about the properties of marriages
that rely on temerity and laconic lies to survive.

I overhear a bruised neighbour call it pain redress,
while another names it *manji*-pleonasm, desire
inescapable as they slowly circle half-bled *lik-kiep*,
relocated narcosis and promise. I try to piece together
the confusing sounds sweeping back and forth
before me. A woman pushing a stroller stops,
telling me how strange it is to move so far
to Canada and still end up in the *Namib* desert.

My hypochondriaxles roll, panicked at feelings
of isolation in a folded city, growing with each
anæsthetic moan. I remember *ah-poh* telling me not
to mistake resuscitative breathing for mere CPR, like
the time she was scared when a giant grouper swam up
beside her, its pectoral fins the same size as her
flippers, dark body heavily scarred like the
three-inch lotus hooks she listened for as a child.

I see her again, weaving through a loud mass of Chinese
cyclists, thumbing tinny handbar bells, touching or
knocking strangers down with shoulder-pole loads.
She stops and takes my hand as I move from the tree,
making the noise of the grouper opening its mouth,
exposing rows of gill rakers. Cleaner shrimp and
wrasses listen for a yawn from the carnivore's mouth,
a signal to enter.

Lui kou ying

She hears the squeak of alloy wheels
along a narrow track
row of taut skinless bodies
still warm on metal hooks
snout roughly removed
for being too white with PSS
hydrous pattern of fervid calyces bluster
from inmost carcass like the kangaroo rat
– urine so dense it crystallizes hitting carmine air –
her eyes like lidded wells
each blink holding warm summer rain

When she gathered stones
from the river to make stupas
first storey for her mother
second for saddened twin brother
third stone returned to river
When father took *Xishi*
crying to the hospital
When sand fleas had so grown in her feet
she could no longer dubbin-walk to
sister who secretly wished
she was born a lost *mabiki* baby

She tensed at the thought of knife
and iodine on paws
but father did not return with the sow
claiming it was just not *chih-te*
like his eleven-year-old blind daughter –
widow-whore's *kuo*
wrinkled fast by tongues

Her youth worth remembering
a charming toddler small enough
to hide under one of his scales

when he recited *The Wood Scripture*
to rebuild her arthritic leg

Woke each day
bracing pain in thighs
recalling Xishi's *longzhu* eyes
that saw her face roil and churn
in hypnomonotony as she chewed lunch
in rumour-refrain school

They noticed lickety sounds in her uniform
as she stuck their tongues as far down
her throat as she could stretch
minds who refused to see *Cockayne*
creeping umbelliforms of *da-ying*
from the last pointed incisor:

Who stole my *nao-ke*-pearl?

Defenceless

i don't mind the cold of a recombinant dream
where nothing furred, feathered or haired
moves in past-forward ...

For the longest subaperture second, you squat three miles up from the beach. Talking to a stream that is 112° Fahrenheit in the breeze, full of giant four-headed golden carp and cyclopean turtles, you receive no response, like jerking off to the test pattern post-*Baywatch*.

Gluing apart another neon Jesus wristwatch with eyes that follow you wherever you go, you wonder when you can afford matching DD-xenotransplants. Television overbombs mind, distracted from *brahmacharya* and constant muted sound of humanure falling into itself.

Having only one finger left on either hand, he unsuits the skeletons he imagines want to use her body, including the *mudhawallah*, calling his wares while cycling past. It slips out, all the while swearing at pre-sated *Chinnamasta* loins.

You dimly remember a home where mother called you *chen-jen* in your pressed fetal dress, before crying at the traces of a practiced hand. Running, you wanted a shredded in-tray of those penises from the view of satellite altimetry: not even dots.

You heard what could happen to women possessed by labial ghosts. The bored pathologist fits a circular clamp around a dead woman's skull, removing her brain – a puddle of blood poured into his *heh ko* sample, dusted with a haze of fine white bone meal.

You feel him slice Mother's 'sick' brain into thick slabs that tumble like the traffic in cheap radioactive religious icons from Chernobyl. I have abseiled your head without fear. Waiting by nuke-water, we are startled by the wakeful song of the last *baiji, kala*.

Beatroots

She calls on a cloud to wring a strange applause of rain
over the paddle mark between the eyes. Hurt
by silence, co-creators think: *ugly,* twiddled knobs
for ears like old mother's crumpled bodice and belly folds.

Whisper-whipped and reviled after three sets
of fingertip whorls rustled love's lure. Gums on nipples
during wet minutes, enjambed line by line of *hello,*
before air-browsing lips fell silent on sheetside placentæ.

Beyond the blackened fields, trailing blankie, she licks
the cloth and savours the blood.
Euphoriant and emetic, a shrunken bush
sops up her tears, falling by the quart, as she buries the dead.

With a single orphaned potato, thieved for the last thing
said of her, *you must be juz ...* she answers the silence
with poofed breath, *ahh-oohs, lafa, do you yooth?* and
a creed of screams that could settle the mills.

Pleading for food from the priest, she chokes on
communion wafer with each heave of pellucid desire.
Lifting biretta, he wipes his saltwash sap from
her back, sharing the moistness of decaying blanket.

Aurora hour iterates corky rot in the fields, while
hunger roars polymath pain that coats her door
in bastard umber. Opens to a bulge of boozy
complex sugars, lies that fit between the rain.

Too weak to rage at the bleached clay he wears,
she cries a little, milk-substantial, thinking it will spoil
in his mouth. She makes a rasp, tottering against the pulse
of ant-shrapnel on forgotten faces, bonneted in history.

Inky jackals file her womb under conjugal mastery.
Sugared umbilici reach for a head against a tuber mound.
Time-pocked insistences plant a calabash, root-willed like
the wanted posters on each face, the suppliance of lodging
and departure.

Ride

switched on
recorder listens
jerks open briefcase
lipsynching remains
snaps it shut
paces under skylight
slubs and rips in panty
build patch of finish
where subjoined silence
clads the faultless lover

scrumpy touch
of rasp and whipcord
scrapes against jodhpurs
he rips it to ankles
in double-locked livery
bidding equine croup
with Morris slapper
leaping backward
in the winking light

shakes off midden efflux
sprayed on riding boots
before massaging
calomel conditioner behind ears
moving unsteadily
on black bars of high heels

one foot in stirrup
he spirals in mid-air
detaches saddle
exposing fur back
bare for biddable kisses
pubic sweat epigraphs
hairy toes rub against flat tops

falling in front of its start
on the pig bladder
tangled in sticky stocking tops
his fingers strapped
her cheeks bone-tight
pulling her hair like reins
he rode her face
while she giggled
at the infield flies
amber to heavy
the gelid tip of his cock

tensely tabulating
the price of being the fool
outsize hankies
leather hockey sticks
swipes of safe-home instructions
wondering
if love will come for him

in the crush of hooves
poised before a feeble light
seeing her somewhere
closing in

Fat

Home from the humane society,
she carries striped orange cat. Bushy array
of whiskers, the false moustache
of a roving bandit in somnopolis alleys.
Gentle hands cage her with pending hope,
gingerly eating the apple.

Ninety-three pounds, eyes like silver helium
pinpricks, shining through surrounding
flesh in anatomized flight. Placing cat
in front of a lasagna platter. Face-off.
Cat sniffs it and curls her whiskers away.
Not Garfield. She follows programmed path
to urinal-side scale, with corrugated moods for company.

Names it portion, account-keeping christenings
on the margin of the scale. No menses
for three months. Step routine thirty times a day,
woozy on the arabesque of maroon gym bag,
always the same scroll of doc's pink slips,
direct diary with its vomit lei steering to a buffet.

Stares at two runnels of beer from the
Pacific basin, Kirin and Tsingtao running on tap.
Sorority sister finishes a dish of onion rings,
hot drinks on sterling trays, watermelon
ripe to the wraith's hyperbole. Beside her, a dirty table
near the edge of chalcedony precipice
wound with veins that swallow everywhere at once.

Starting on baked beans, bag poised on her
lap to catch any tumbling idea. Scoops a teaspoon
of cat food into the bowl, relief-pitcher paw reaches
for the wedge. Rolling on her back, frontispiece
scratched with razor blades, articulated bones,

breakable, unnerved numbers of whiskers.
Short-order on all sides, she displays her teeth
as for the vet, measuring their hard sigh ten times.
Pucks the plate across hardwood toward goalie,
taking off the #10 blazer. The sun gone
down, darkness like the inside of a licorice jelly bean.
Ceiling fan to a vision of handlers laughing
at her thighs elongated in the water. No word
for the sound a spring-long splash is.

Crawls underneath the comforter, warms
distended bladder and colon. Sloshing of the
candy tomorrow. Crusted brain doesn't
notice the snow piling deeper. Rummaging
for the ice the grader has missed: love's agent
attacking a hungry stomach.

Permanently spry waves fallen, occasional phlegm
puddle, four whiskers lost in as many hours, portion
closes her eyes on the street. Summer night shovels
split-ended hair clusters into the wind: a game
in which fat leftovers become the bubbled God
in the glare of a hospital room, not the vermiform heat
of *gloop gloop gloooop gross*, heard from
sleepy forms in front of the fridge at three am ... Ocean.

Thin. Nobody calls her that on the calendar
dumpscape. No beauty contests for human insides,
scansion on a single waitress serving episodic again.
Looks in a mirror in the morning, frowning at her
nude body. Underspace of the buttocks like the
trampolinist when she drops. Notices cat, some
mixture of missing in the marble-hearted city.
Follows the gradual dissolve of paw marks to ...

Lout resolve weaker than the palest ooze, spelling fat
on the clerestory window, lined up, single file, nine cats

before her eyes, each feeding on the next.
Groom kisses bride's cheek, the disobedient dance
of baby dimple parts them again. Portion
approaches and risks licking out the snarl
of whisker in her eyes. By and by, seeing nobody
close, she outsizes the lonely stand of the goddess
on the tap, steadying her mouth for self-reproof.

Serration

You walk once over a thick sheet of glass covered by stippled paper, the old pedobarograph producing a picture of pressure. The isobars beneath your heels are a series of concentric near-circles, circumpolar like the spring day you took me for a walk in Strathcona Park, where we stopped under a tree. You carved a small hole that seemed to breathe like a stoma with the voice of an electronic larynx. Barely able to stand, you told me about the importance of killing to overcome the pain of knowledge, the never-known and its echo.

You fed the small gopher peeping in our heat-prostrated nights, quaking about the dangers of chlorofluorocarbons and the likelihood of China's copycat industrial growth, leading to two trillion cigarettes a year and cancer like a hatched atom as big as immortality. We are ruining Canada, eh? An easy going nation unwilling to consider a visit by *sin nombre* across its border, giving the gopher his due in futurology. Descending on a prayer-wheel getaway, the soil carried her off to marry earth anew each morning, handing you sanctuary.

Shortly after waking, you notice the gopher standing upright. Its shoulders shrug with each musical groan of the old forest. Playful, it approaches you. Scraps of food fall from invaginated cheeks, just so. You lift a bolt-action Remington .22, barely noticing the dull thud as a bullet slams into its soft underparts. The animal rears and touches you in falling. You turn back to your paper in the same breath, seeking the principle of transmittable death in the spasm of lips saying *no* to your draughty heart.

Because of love, you explained, the jumping blood that assumes a permanent place in a small second of what is remembered and never learned, when you assume there is no god available for rescue purposes from an economy of pain, where simple creatures live in everlasting ambush. A praying mantis lands on your laptop and you grab a magnifying glass to watch as you trap it under the rim of a glass. The only insect that can turn its head looks you in the face with mettlesome eyes, and you halve its trunk, laughing at its wings unshackling as they fall by the edge of my throat.

Noisily excited about the discovery of fluid used to freeze rat brains. Reheated and resuscitated, undamaged, you wonder if they can still think. The implications are obvious, or so you feel, with switchback secrets that crack the stone of my lungs. Torqued motor stops, leaving the miracle of an ampersand in wet earth when we parted. On theetiquette of tea with the lost ark, I picked out the slackskin rats that came out of your mouth, as if you already lived in a tomb, hiding the body to come.

Seezure

Let's do it. In any case, it's better than dying at his hands ...
– Excerpt of a confession from Yang Jinying (1452)

Shadow-boxing trencherman fritzes off 3.2 pounds
worth of calories from her red lollipop,
discards beside the teeter-totter, half-suckled.
Her outline splits his universe
as he watches from the car.
Sugar-coated rod singes tied tongue
as he muses how moisture inside
the windshield works to conceal
his stare at fifty feet. But she always *knows*,
squints to see who's pretending
to idle. Sailor Moon comb falls
from miniature knapsack
and she bends carefully to pick it up.
His gastric juices do a jailhouse jig – spewage as he
stares at legs and their slim-skipping
speed. Primordial predator/prey repose
to desire is the prelude to
attack from behind, snapping her spine
with a single kiss.

He remembers his own mother, angry
that the kids of his father's friends
monopolized the TV, kept him from watching
his favourite show.
'Why is it better for three people to be selfish
than for one?' She ignored him.
He peed and shat all over the linoleum,
ran to the neighbour's house
to watch their TV, his sometime babysitter
quickly switching from the image
of a tongue on a hairless pearly bivalve.

The video back on, he settles
on a floppy chair, asks the sitter to turn
off the yucky stuff before noticing warm fingers
moving up the nape of his grubby neck.
He twitches the hand away in half-dread as the sitter
ejects the tape, muttering about the sweet
briny taste of gamine morellos under tropical sun.
Returning home at the end of the show,
the seams and creases of his palm reappear
on his body as his father berates him.
At every word he falls on a single knee and emits
the metallic moans of the video girl
who looks like one of his brainy classmates with braces.
Peering back, he wonders if she will approach or run.

She recalls her mother's true bedtime story about brave
live-action figurines, replaying their lives
as killers in order to survive. The game began when Yang
prepared a silk cord, while Yao made a noose,
as Xing covered his face with thick yellow fabric
and Liu pinned down his legs, watching the Chinese
Crested hump his helpless limbs with happy abandon.
Homicidal *candiru* eyes
watching young bodies swim naked,
pissing at his command as they swam.
Tiny fish following golden streams
stick out sets of painful spines.
Surgeons were not called. The emperor liked
the look of fused faces before bladders burst in his bed
and they lay dead.

She runs and tells.

Wandering Song

For Edmond Yu

Spiderwoman and Laceman caress in lookout, papery bodies beside the skyline swine who plonk Tetris headblocks over their monodist cardboard mobile. They talk about the melamine messengers who left deep hoofprints in the snow as they hijacked Santa's sleigh. Crashing through the Eaton Centre, they leer at its transparency, a continuous display of motionless windows, escalators, water fountains and glass doors. A child comes out of the matinee during winter to find the day almost over. Hurtling an inch from the shriek of some untrodden brake, she returns home to count how many times she tried to run away this year, now thinking things would be better at Christmas, hunkered into a fetal bulb under the tree.

She could hear both singing and crying through the shower curtain, repsycling the fear of his return to fill their stockings in rubbered red, agleam with a post-coital sheen. He chuckles over sugar-plum fairies intercepted by *Hypnos* who watched him knock over the warm milk in his haste to play bezique with her little pair of hearts, shaking as she maunders herself out of a nightmare (she was choking up a poinsettia plant, carpel mettle mangled at the roots by empty cookie plate). She keeps hearing *Ho! Ho! Ho!* while singing in music class after the holidays. The teacher places a hand on her sternum, observing how her ribs do not move. *Do you think of your ribs as a cage?* she says. *Instead, think of them as shiny gills,* while all she can focus on is drowning beneath his ice lolly.

Heading for Harbourfront on the Spadina bus, she walks past a sweet-faced woman yelling, *I'll kill you ya motherfuckah* ... Another woman screams for methadone, and she sees a man waving a small tabla hammer. He incants: *hello/kayotsarga/uh/shake/cup/uh* ... Nonsensical, she thinks, until she notices his hand movements with the hammer, tapping intricately against nothing but the aviary hum of failing voices on a cold street, prying her spirits apart. She follows him to the Scott Mission where a worker tells her she should see the smiles that emerge from when a hairdresser volunteers to come in, just because someone's touching him. She wanders home and, seeing mother tap lightly around the rims of the drum using a tabla hammer to restore its tonal explorations, smiles. The skins get too loose.

Hope Holds

for the repose of Edward Bak (1934-1997)

You don't make a sound, shielding your face with your hands as you stare at me behind the crook of your elbows. I am frightened of you, but you insist on hiding from me. My rebounding carcass remains torn each time I try to see the love that drills its stylet into my heart. I was born with the word *ah-bah* on my lips, before I learned to talk. Our red brick house a home where the bathroom tiles hid nether burglars underneath the bathtub and dark ghosts under the hardwood floors. Brick by quarrelsome brick, I imagine the house melting slowly into the sea. A *grilse* nudges at the door and you let it in, assured that it will swim happily through the serum inside that drowns out the pain. You left and I stayed, wondering why.

Three or four times a year I would get a raging sore throat which registered in my neck as a field full of crows, and you would offer me a bite of your apple. I called *Daddeee!* when a bee bit me on my thumb. You ignored me until I was so annoyed with the crows' relentless cawing that I began cawing back, imitating their sounds and enjoying the feeling it created in my throat; the soreness diminished until you walked away again, closing off my windpipe in a one-way ratchet. Sputtering sobs,I waited for you to return, relaying spinneret messages to protect me from from the lewd clamour of your other life, disjoining us.

There's no way of telling how many times I wished you could know that my silence operates at multiple levels of meaning, as much as my speech. I hid in a nearby lo-fi recording studio, enjoying a loud share of detuned guitars, undermiked drums and continual hiss. I hid in the public library to learn what really happened to Bambi's mother: led into a small stall and pummelled on the head with a pneumatic hammer gun and within three minutes she has been bled and skinned. I hid in your empty room when you were gone, retracing the imaginary animal friends you encouraged me to draw on you, which I prayed would never go extinct. You readily agreed.

Double-duty turntablist that you are, you worked longer and longer days against the lurching and crashing voices in your head, telling you to leave out the spacy treble for hardened repetitive bass against the disconstancy of money and its disbanded reverie of broken hearts, flanged to effortless hope. Quickly made the necessary pit stop back to Kingston. My fingers linger on the toilet handle, which feels for an instant like the twin curve of your free-floating *hyoid* and the warm vibrations in the front of your neck. Slowly adducing an unanswerable question to the little fish that tries to heal your fevered forehead by kissing it all over lightly before flowing away, leaving detailed patterns of pain in the water as it swims from its home, elapsing with the memories when you are not there, living, somewhere, dying, or in here, holding me.

Shine Swing

plastic tag moves around her neck
with a large number eight on it
so it can be easily identified
through neon hassle shower

drug-limned eyes in the room
follow her bored gyrations
barely feeling the contours of their laps
on her bare *chelonian* buttocks

  mind wanders to the mothballs in the closet
  mother sleep-talking
  with the voice of Deuteronomy 22:21
  advises stoning until welts appear
  on her back

  a dropped loonie jolts her drapery of dengue
  as she notices another *farang* tour group
  salivating through Patpong
    she can never hear her own heart

        focuses instead on
  the curious relation
  between the shells under her pillow
  and the little stolen pistol in her hand
        imagines the linking of arms
  to form a sheath of blood
  stockpiling closure over neglected feelings
  and with a cry the room of girls following her

        while she waits for another kind of touch
        behind a hundred-foot high-plate-glass window

heavy makeup drips on her sister's vomit
before the misprision of night

tries to fuck herself ahead
of the successive darkness
and its lambent incline

sun hauls itself up
weaving light on a gurney
between her thighs
after eight inbound erections in a row

before breaking into church
to steal and gorge
from the pyx
without swallowing to adore it
she senses a sickness that
sees and hears

the smell of the sagging wooden floor
under the weight of motorcycles
inchoate machines in a poor life
where both angel and diabolus
oversleep in industrial turd piles

under the shadow of great Siam kings
and her grandmother's bile ranch
where she sends tip money
to feed the household heroin habit
that brings skeletons back to life
like the turtle heads without appendages
transfusing blood into the rim
of each other's stumps

the cash always arrives half way
through a show featuring fifteen varieties of poisonous snakes
skilfully nurtured from the nearly vanished forest
where her school was burned down
leaving the *xulan* standing in the ashes

slashed bark like the sticky prominence
of illegal loggers creeping around his daughter
    his sadness when he sold her
to escape fields which no longer spoke green
                guarded poppy farms nearby
                take on the aftermath of rape like stickpin worms

                after cramming 600 *baht* into bag
she runs with the flaring growth of light
believing the client who just sat   and spoke
through a beard like mountain-goat wool
that turned into fog, revealed a touch
that could hold fear in abeyance
    in clairvoyance

    carries her secretly to the *thoms*
queued to kiss the feet
of the ill, recircled in a touch
    she thinks of them like the derelict nuns
whom she idolized in her village, strong enough
to crease their eyes like flickknife fists
as they conversed with the dying
and chased down their terror

                head in the fan of a warm bosom
steady though her legs were blown off
by an unseen device in the dirt
they moan as she swallows snake bile
and shakes as it mixes
with the taste of transactions with men
who said they loved her before they paid
but left her with nothing

gilding in deposits of tears
over a criminal presence
which calls her *norng yai.*

she never held still long enough
to notice the swinging sound
reminding her to inhale negative
while exhaling positive

    when the stake was planted upright
    through her body, eyes cast down
    another bloodstain
    below the darkness of the first

another claret drip grieves the changeless child
the fresh hole in the ground
dug by disordered love, the violent sound
of the beloved
before a final goodbye

                lovesick and hideous
the moon playing at landfall
when she undoes the back eyehook
on her left stocking   cranes over
to find a set of chipped nails
pulling it gently down from below

a signatory kiss comes from
bending harder into prayer
    the lush bræ that savours
the green taro, dangling disguised
and swollen in early fall
    an immaculate dream of coupling
    the divinity that dons a face

                they ignite the open window
    and adhere to each other's skin
    arrayed for *bardo*-shine
                they dance to a crimson trail
    testing the last bed for comfort
    above the sunset
        a moment of light

Superstar

Shaking manicured hands gauge my temperature when I lose count of the missing stars in the pavement of Hollywood Boulevard. They ascend and combust above loud tourists and rice-paper snareplanes. I fly into the Baroque retable. On the fiery set, it stands, obstinate, waiting – and I only care about letting it die.

Ai ya ... hot word, she says before leaving me with a miscued cold grip trace to go shopping for fangs. She re-enters carrying a bottle of pink cough syrup and another unwanted business card from a guy who claimed to be a studio exec, staggering like a poolside tapir, snorting a long line of broad-scale history. Nose leaks a four-count bleeding cycle on another cock as surgical stitches slacken from yesterday.

She imagines for a moment her exhausted jaw rolling under a diner voice-box before coming to rest on a neon porn marquee. Contracting her masseter muscles, she stands silently, watching as he unzips. This one smells. He pays her to listen as he calls himself *Sterilox*, jerking off toward the dark patches between gibbering stars.

Above the noir steam vents between LaBrea and Sycamore, she wonders if she will ever have a star in the asphalt like *Anna May Wong*, 1960. On Hollywood contract to act unfailingly di-visible, she stole a boat loaded with rich clothing, dumping it all like wan petals before the vulgar, wealthy and white.

Don't cry ... don't cry, she tells herself in the dead building. A scatter of roles lost for lack of accent and too few tongue tricks. The fast-acting sweepstake in the room looks away as she puts her mouth to the floorboards and talks to the piebald terrier downstairs. Both share anger at the point of entry to a success-or-die world, without a decolouring book for beginners.

She heats plain congee, crouching again to say good night to the dog, convinced it feels abandoned, like the three-legged puppy she left in China. Howling, she shares electric surges for an hour, while a comfy crowd laughs as its fur is seared off. She can still hear it barking at every audition, knowing spectators pay big bucks for a cold bowl of her thigh in *youngyangtang*. With the *erhu* tucked between her legs, she swallows a string of menstrual sarsen during *song hezi*.

Captious halves waved goodbye as she boarded an America-bound ship. Fantasy-crutched, she acted aloud with blood-cloth mask, starting on B-flick motets to gangster bel cantos. On to comedic dirges as she flips Egg McMuffins like a herd of men trucked in from basic design.

I wake in the morning to find a note from her, leaving early to capture the Starship Enterprise, boldly going where no Asian woman has gone before. The dog begins to cry the long-tailed tune of a *ku-ch'in*, taking the spotlight like an Anatolian Karabash and her shadow, weighing well over 100 lb at ten years in the casting circuit. She launches into *Queen Thiang's song*, left out of the film:

Western people funny, Western people funny, Western people funny,
of that there is no doubt,
They feel so sentimental about the Oriental,
They always try to turn us inside down and upside out ...
They think they civilize us,
Whenever they advise us,
To learn to make the same mistake,
That they are making too! ...

She returns with a contract like a wild east sword-swinger, with a blanched stammer of excitement, *I think I got a knack for this shit*. The dog quiets as it takes a swig of penny-prayers she has hoarded as ambition, reconquest. Her slanted eyes on the sidewalk resemble annelids when they heal in the prolapse of fallen stars. Near a closed Texaco station off Hollywood Boulevard, she fuels a dream by cutting her *fengchi* ... gathering a million windsongs to show everyone how to spot a lady who bows to endings, unknowable.

Eruption

The street is where people stroll in time, wait for lovers, park for food, run into friends, take on guardian corners ... but the street is not her lost life, income-static among shoppers. She is sure that her gemless wedding ring is tinged with 'Fidelidad,' though she can't remember to who. She wants to fly back on the wings beneath her raggy layers, but to where? Behind a mirage of ice-bead curtains, snowstorm globes of constant Christmas and glowing rosaries, she sells for loose change or trades sex for smack like the other glamazons, who always manage to philosophize about whether shelter or badly defined regulation can stop the graves that run like jagged duelling scars under plush antechambers. A fever foundation helps her swallow the cheap drugs she feeds herself, under the hoax of tuna (69 cents a can), all the while cursing politicians like Tsubouchi. Clone-sprouting a meaty glaze on their foreheads as they quicken the lie circuit, they remain entranced by their own unavailing egos, ignoring the wriggling bodies swelling under each manhole in the megacity. Like cherries dried to transparency, in the mote-hung nights, she says: *We shall sink together, you and I ...*

> *Push-pack*/a small woman who wakes for a second, dressed in a long navy blue coat that covers her body on the bench. Only the white hair suggests a human, they think, even as her head twitches up. A last wish for a trusted hit that knows why dreams become printing blocks, doubling in space before you notice the hard stop.
>
> *Underthrust*/a boy who has been ditching school for three weeks after being called *faggot* by some suits and then beaten at home for being underemployed, wonders if the first penis he allows in his mouth for cash is a worm which needs continual moisture as it respires through its skin. He carefully wipes off the sour stuffing, hoping to dry it out so it cannot spit in him again.
>
> *Upwelling*/a widow in Little India sadly prepares her daughter to turn a trick for the first time. A closed-drawer story helps. *King Satakarni Satavahana of Kutala* killed his verdant wife with a pair of scissors because she could not sustain *Indrani* after he came once. She ends with the advice to just lie still with her fear, hideways.

Pulling on and off a half-exorcised smile, she opens another new $3.25 box of Holiest Water Fountains in the shape of the Blessed Virgin Mary. Says nothing while shivering for a good twenty minutes, opening and closing a squeaky Mary fan so rapidly that an image appears in the creases, like the sacred art that showed semen emanating from

God's mouth and passing through a long tube that led under Mary's dress. She rocks on her heels, caught in the tussle of grief counselling herself.They never bother to take off their dull three-piece suits with the shiny gold Tory pins on the lapels before stretching her legs into the Japanese character for 'man.' She staggers on a round of sudden cues, a laugh about *yobai* politicians, a bloodshot streak of tea, a hankie over internment –

Buried under beds of lava, memory burns up the best-known in her. Stares at a crumpled tag. It reads: *I'm a Catholic. In case of accident or illness please call a priest/pusher.* She can't tell the difference as she staggers to Queen's Park, stopping to caption each vomit-twist, *Fuck* without warning, fatigue overruns memories and she wakes to find blood. Her unfitted diaphragm hangs with a vicious cramp. Sudden snow turns the lumps into a rusty red gale between her hands, then onto the government steps. The blood dissolves under the patient licking of heaven's tongue, and a low rumble follows each minister who leaves the building. Their legs give way as if summoned to fall across her anger. Splatter on cement, an omen like a clot of porter-flies at the edge of overdosed eyes. Fears of plugged magma chambers under the city, an enormous subduction of blood entering their billfolds, strong enough to unroof every house on the holiday eve, fire the sleigh's rudder to rush out dream stubs for the next shaky act. Resting her back on a rod of light beside a gaping crater, she is alone, knowing that no one can legislate the dark.

Enough

impassable
the blend of will
in a single mind
two planes push overhead
    stubborn Siamese fighting fish
inside her wombwater spasm

love slides onto separate sodden clouds
that allow the rain to fall
in her bruised arbour
    conjoined at their small heads
albumen scabs
growing from her gutsack
heart-hold of calm
tractable across her cheek

she rolls them together
    birdlike demurrals lodged inside
    refolded compressed intestinal coils

filled with a tailwind of nausea
she is tired of watching the patent snits
and self-serving scandal
of amateur actors and pro confessives
    trying to give their lives
    a new magnitude of reality through TV talk
    like there's no power in privacy
    by the end-to-end of our beds

she cracks the screen
tired of fitting between pearly tiles
the fire on the stove picks up the paint job
tired of the steady pulse of commands
pushing a logic of global occupation
like a child's trustful glide

on an airport carousel
as though it carries bags full of toys
instead of wannabe work and
saleable misfortunes

she drinks from his coffee cup
lets it slide from her hands
  fragments snag at her feet
a sugar lump under her shoe
  the shorter leg of her chair
  disintegrates entirely

she falls at his concussive frequency
or it could be follow-up fear
takes out a tray of fresh bread
combining figures in an assortment
of rings and awls that break
like lifting lead
in her spit backup

  servation returning in an hour
  she jigs the valance above the window
  but it scutters off on its own
  to land over the door

things around the house
stimulate the love-rigged shadows
caught running
on the black exhaust of rejoined promises

she worries that her vulva is a loudmouth
  the ache in her back a pistol barrel

he climaxes in the moral scour of possession
nodding off to the unchange of goodbyes
tied to free-range pincers to stay

for the topnotch loneliness
apologies
forcing a focus
the way he tines her return
on the dog-legged stair
    ejecting rage
    arced through the air on half-landing
    each *puh leez* pares away its leather holder
    empty bottle bobs down his throat
    bullets like metal pasties over breasts

she kneels on the floor shaking
he pitches badly in the air
turning her over and over on his tongue
    her fear becomes a nameplate
that traps his hands in the bedroll

he lets her down and hands it to her
expecting tit-for-tat
before the door skids over
and she leaves a supple stand-in
hand soap in the stairwell

stands to the side of his closing eyes

Manga-Doll

She opens a well-worn *yon-kama manga* and runs her eyes one-way afterword off the page ...

1 Stumbling stout under billboard subvertisement that he altered to say pre-opening over used white panties. Strokes his unkempt beard, softly comical, borrowed from Jim Henson's Creature Shop. Enters his favourite store for *ero-manga*, gaping lips exposing a tongue like a radula. Engrossed with a page featuring gangsters poking guns up blanked-out vulvas, he pretends not to notice his newly teened daughter in the background, climbing down from a highrise pappus of hair.

2 After playing pat-a-cake with his skinsumptive shadow, she sprayed her geisha doll's hair into a rigid taxidermied hive. She repeatedly re-counts a 10,000-yen tip before squashing it in her kitty bank. A post-test bonus in exchange for an hour of touching under her white starched shirt, hand vanishing and reappearing like a command-composed ghost.

3 Thrum-wrapped, she feels the weight of the claw hammer between the toes of her immaculate white tabi socks. Her body gave involuntary shivers when her father allowed one of his old *chigoe*-friends, a prison escapee, to finger her like a flageolet. For over a year he'd watched purple blemishes develop on his penis, which he rubbed too hard against the unseemly crevices of the locks – hand cupping a key, plucking at nothing. Bits of lust on her Posturpedic attaches to song, a wife's telling of rape-dolphin, cool to her diary.

4 Foreplay for the real struggle. He tightens the cord around her neck, and her mind flashes to the wish-songs of the pretty middle-aged women with their faces powdered to pallor rather than the creamy blank white of the high-end *ryotei*. She graciously pours sake for an assigned businessman, her nails curled into hookworms. Her face has the eerie silence of a toy fitted with a heart moving in three dimensions, arms attached too far apart to undo a noose. All the bones gesturing inside her uniform, motored by ions from a doll's comb, flapping into the comical venation of Tokyo.

Polylogue Promise

for Frantic

You appear to me

... scuba diving in aqua regia with visor smile, coral blowing mutely in your ear. There is no true thing between us. Your words ward off the storms on my long search for the last *ying lian*, as I hang on the ledge of the CN Tower's rotation, blind to the human strobe lights below.

... roaming through the incense of summer grasses, sweeping your bare bruised legs against knee-high rattles. You recall the green of the *bayul*, a band of metamorphic rock twisted into the shape of a cobra, head drawn back to frighten. Your hands shaking in divested clarity.

... in a riverside scene by Seurat, where you lie under the purple sky. With a sense of cæsura and distance, you recognize the girl, the blood of stewing hens on her soft arms, outfacing the clouds. She was you, before my father re-readied himself for physical apoplexy and emotional apostasy. In a shrinking landscape, cum is squared by uneven hands.

... as a conchologist, who can crack my shell of self-consumption. Behind the neo-Gothic grotesquerie of the bar, we watched drunken patrons with lit red candles stuck to their heads and shoulders, guessing which ones would stick out their tongues to catch the drops.The nail punctures our spreading belief in a stop-motion ripple – you astride the nightingale, dripping pizza oil on my windowsill.

... in my most secret dreams, as a wolf, stronger off Prozac, you lope through the streets in filched clothes, prepensive in locating the limits between your own body and the *feng huang* I try to conjure in my black box bag. It unnames every passage of fixative pain, like the shapes a flock of birds make, trusting the wind warder to free love, where you think

you aren't missed

Twin-Squatting

It was always cold in the unheated theatre, a porn house on weekends. The girls stood about in yellow blancmange leotards. Of course, they were not dancers at all, but scabrous reminders of childhood, unfaded even after her sister disappeared.

Their mother, who could barely distinguish between them, told them that a poor woman's cumwork is never done, then demanded that they become women early, in the money bower, where they say the devil never wears out his cock.

Hematuria started to give up smoking at twelve by limiting the matches, swallowed while she stared out the window. She hardly noticed the rhythmic trundling of her body under another, wishing to be like the cylinder of wire netting put up to protect a young tree, feeling the dull ticking of the adding machine calling them again. She stared back at the stars, so many eyes peeping from the dripcastle sky. The paper goddess cried like microwave popcorn, her gown edges puckered and ashen, a paper crane upended in the folds. Its tail burned hot, flaming up the dress of silence she carries in her mouth.

Anhedonia saw a swing when she turned fourteen, eighty-eight seconds before her sister. She didn't share how its top was flush with the clouds. The suspension ropes dangled loose; nobody was playing on it, so she approached it. She swung forward into the rude volley of calf-eyed children. She swung backward into the flaps of their over-bright jowls.

Life resembled a speeding tube train with the driver slumped over the lever, station after station flashing by. Life stopped when it reached the guide-line goddess in the Plaza de Toros, who even tried to show her how to grip a bull's horns and swing up and over each time, propelled by the jerk of the animal's head.

One entered the house and found her pale sister in pyjamas of parachute silk, soaked in a pool of blood. Lips lifting off from a scream, looking like a punctured petunia or the doddery hearts of Eng and Chang, spectacular twins born too close.

The chink-chink-chink of a chisel on the gravestone. Her goddess vanished behind a backdrop of stitched cloudbanks, right after she ran away from the suburban home, under cover of the arborescent city. Twinned faces nesting with the rumbirds, singing in pairs at each antedawn.

Wake-Walking

She sat down again at the rectangular formica table
in the kitchen, old willow still weeping like
the pillow she seldom slept on. Growing up
she marvelled at how the willow's roots appeared
so strong by day they made the walkway buckle
at night.

In the bath, she saw an extra pair of eyes, a stiffened face
next to her own soapy visage. Standing on tip toe
like a cartoon burglar, he paused after each step
toward the door. She wondered why he did not walk loudly,
since he was asked to come, to steal the impression of
open legs.

Transceiving shapes from his ventriloquist dummy's head
with a visible *Kirlian* aura, she saw his wet towel
turn into a magic carpet. The dream-genie
poured a cascade of iodine onto a cottonball cloud
to clean her cuts
                                        after throwing the man from
the balcony.

She listened to footsteps that never approached or receded
into the distance, as they should have done; no walk
that paused to insert feelers like those of a barbel, no sign
of teeth in its mouth. Creases on both sides of her face
as though she'd been sleeping hard before she woke
on her feet.

Dropped Back

We arrived at the dining hall where the *p'i-p'a* concert was about to start. The room dark and empty except for a luminous loophole. A bloodless face says *Can you stand these bright sea-urchin eggs on me?* Old woman, sitting still, looked like *Yee Poh* with a kermes whelk over her head. Is this a pancestral ghost?

We climbed into the car. A red warning light on the dash stayed lighted. *Kung Kung* told me the generator wasn't producing enough energy to keep the battery charged, and we would be robbed of power soon. The steering wheel was entwined with dead orchids. I slumped in my seat and piped, *Maybe this is a goer.*

I stepped out of the car to make for the phone booth, before hearing the sound. A glance backward revealed the old woman picking pocketfuls of ramen noodle. How many ways can a hand close around itself, grasping some sad thing too soon felt? *Wansee-wansee*, nearing the coiled core of the soft-shelled claw, a ring rattled for his finger in a street buffet.

The car started. At home, his head turned this way and that, surrounded by a kitchen reliquary of bones and snapped roots, gills opening and leeching the ring. It drank dizzily against his fingers. Watching the clean motion, he wondered why it pushed against the flaccid flesh, where it didn't want to go.

The oven popped open to a thigh-high pie. Humming the '*Red Rose Three Wishes*', a song he played to her while rice rode weepy blankets, he stole her jade necklace during a well-fed goodbye. Yee Poh lost his baby – her uterus was heart-shaped rather than the normal pear shape. *Heck gai shee*, he said, leaving her corpse reshaping a garbage heap.

She took soft soap and stuffed it into the holes in her gums, silent hinges of age. In her street suite, there is the lifting of one food package and another. She went after the pool of dried soy sauce, smearing it on him in the skin-warm air of the restaurant, complaining that his hot and mustardy milk hurt her too.

I saw her sitting on a chair with four sticks of dynamite on the legs. After igniting, she rolled herself into a tight ball. The blast hurtled a sticky endocast of truth as her hands papered hornetlike, round and round the strange fish ball on his breath. Airing her arms above the smoke, she kneaded his half-growth of beard. Spiced like equilimbed wicks of explosive, in excellent trim, he stands pretending to have forgotten. Sweating nutrient quick, he saw his arm running east beside her, his fingers closing around a ring lodged in an uneven roundness. Showing one way our bodies unwant us, she disappeared in the glitter of swimming fish elided.

jung

The moon and Pleiades
are set. Midnight,
and time spin away.
I lie in bed, alone.
– Wang Wei

i write
on stretched parchment
retractile brush
and anodyne ink
an interrupted stroke
will break the line
or blur the paper

erasure?

deliberation?

affliction?

impossible

when I fail to communicate
from deep inside my throat
the song of the dents and wears
in a sofa
empty of children

sorrowful
I regard
cryogen popsicles
in my solitary veins
and tender-necked summit

raising arms to ceiling
trying to reach your pacing
pencil screams
into my lungs
    when I feel a cramp in
    the colour of my face
    new to the convulsive sweetness
    of Mr Big on the TV

spurts of milky devotion
poking at odd angles
your scrubbing hands
    cracked with spilt
    dry-cleaning fluid

I hold it right there
in the muscled art
of unleaving

I might take in
the progress of bringing
your body back

sharing a saying
a barely watered kettle
boings over heat

your bosom a just-made bed
where my small breasts
wait immovably

the *jung* feels nothing
but its own
final swelling

no amount of string holds it
    tie harder

harder
make corner tight
so no rice may escape
from a six-hour boil

cover the lotus bud
with fresh bamboo leaves
heal the cuts
with warm sesame oil
and hot water
saved and reused a hundred times
the snarl of bamboo string, in the couch
untangles to clear

the way we go still in the noise
of telling something

chancy bloodstreams
on cinerary stovetop

Black-out

sun's halo in annular eclipse
the white of a huge eye

she scratches it
resurfaces over her
like a black malfocused perfusion

when she was born
the ice loosened
and maple trees oozed sap
woodpecker excavated tree holes
to create flavour-flickering icicles
mother lifted her up
positioning her to suck
the sap at the tip
of an icicle at its sweetest
and she forgot the refraction of herself
wheeze and growl for the first time
at the cold point near her mouth
the small eye of a nautilus
no lens but a pinhole to form
an impatient appeal
back to a full breast
before she woke wrapped in a blanket
abandoned moss agates below
change into the pleroma
of a strange encircling embrace

trying to nap she hears a corncrake
complaining about flying alone
looks over to a kind man
with a pan filled with what looks like twigs
and stagnant water bubbles
crouching menacingly over the fire

he had dropped her off for the first day
of fearful kindergarten yesterday
still not telling her his real name
she learns he makes opium
not with proper poppies
just enough sediment
to keep him disagreeably lost

she stares at him through his stupor
noticing what seem like breasts
bulging from a half-buttoned shirt
she squeezes the inverted left nipple
and the cup of hardened tissue surrounding it
which could easily fit a C cup

    he remained unmoved for an instant
    before beating her in embarassment
    the sting of his hand like the teeth
    of archæopteryx restored in her belly

travelling to Calcutta at twenty when he died
    recurring dreams of a blistery
    patchouli-scented hand that lifted her once
she crawls into a four-and-a-half-foot
concrete pipe like the thousands of others
who use the city's would-be fresh-water pipeline
as cutaway homes

at dusk she counts downturned
paperweight heads like gold-plated records
affixed on the two Voyager probes
images and greetings of life's search on Earth
for someone to hold and infiltrate our fear with love

she feels pain when peeing in the morning
finds an apple-sized abscess growing from her labia
doctor injects an anesthetic into her vagina

she wails each time the scalpel slices the dark cyst
a little dragon with silvery white scales
dashed out of her mouth before she passed out, smiling
her teeth caught a section of the messenger's tail
turning its head back
the dragon was very reluctant

to leave when she returned to Toronto
behind the door
reappearing mother asking for cash and drugs
she leans from the glass
becoming the opaque door without hinges
sealing off the impression of her
as ingrown pastiche of pushful helpmate black-outs

Mina Tulpa

she unlocks the cell and allows the prisoner
to ready for discharge
  instead of the usual asterisk smile of joy
  beckons her inside for a lengthy talk
  about time
    undoing them both like the quiet *mina*
    loud last night
    over furious coughing and screaming fits
      woke her from the warden desk
      never spotting any movement
      from face-down position under the covers
      she snored an unwaking dent into the pillow
      on every flashlight inspection
        convinced the noises were caused
        by atmospheric pressure distorting
        the ticking of the bedside clock
        did not expect to find her sister shivering
        and collapsing on a chair
        refusing to be released in the morning to go home
          to their home near the ærodrome
          where she stood in the flooding basement
          a Disney animatronic figure
          like the Little Mermaid
          caught between a stationary and a moving wall

            she listens, the whites of her eyes
            turning greenish, her head growing
            broader like a blinking lantern on a pole
              receding into the chair she speaks of light
              rejoining a smashed body
              cell by cell in the form of their mother
              encased in the pillow last night
                dressed in glittering layers of metal foil
                that once covered hot in-flight meals
                her head was bleeding in the cockpit

fingers moving like a *cannula*
under her skin to spell remembrance
drained post-flight while the mina managed
to squeeze its way through the prison bars
    they both remember
    how she still flew while lying in the hospital
    a complex tangle of tubes
    entering and exiting her body
    like the sewer rat's bevelled teeth
        doctors extracted a taped roll of bills from
        inside her vagina like Billie Holiday
        hiding twenties to stave off the spectres
        of urban poverty and liver cirrhosis
        circling their home

        returning
            she stares at the grain in the door
            twisting the key in mimicry of her sister
            with proud purpose but reluctant to enter
            another haunted time table prison
                recalls the robber who looked like father
                stealing mother's wedding ring
                newly widowed
                ululating for him in her sleep
                    she scraps her last reserve of crack
                    in favour of the clear haze
                    she sees surrounding an old photo of Mother
                    in a Douglas C-47 spraying thousands
                    of gallons of insecticide at treetop level
                    spelling mass mosquito death
                        while the mina tulpa always survived
                        travelling over a shifting trapezoid of faint lights
                        outlining a liquid hole in a tarn of imagineer sleep

                            radioing her return
                                losing altitude fast
                                crashed into the elusive glow

of release like a *dorado*
    setting a goodbye on the water-clock alarm
    the plane-tail section waving, always
    out of the TV at them in the six o'clock news
    never new

Life To Human

As morning approaches, Chika still hasn't slept a wink as the rain flows into nearby Hanshin subway station. A huge rock falls from the mountain and lands on the injury lab. As researchers yell *mooore money!*, a baboon escapes, head still in a vise, face smashed. Ignoring the flood outside, she zeroes in on the runny splotches on the window, moving with red neon like the cut-and-flash cartoons on TV Tokyo, two flesh creatures fucking, their unhinged lungs bursting from *methyl isocyanate*. Or a sleeping couch potato has his skull opened and injected with a neural siphon rod, not waking even when it goes *bweep* – emptied – you will wake, tireless *bodhicitta*.

The closest she comes to her off-and-on voice sounds like Seska, invoking *Supernaga* to swallow all the negative karma in the power-mad empire. She fears the paralysis of another hour, people standing by, circling the circling of arcuate stitches on the back pocket of the boy who follows the priest down the aisle, swinging the censer, trying to hide the taste of the holy cock still fresh in his mouth.

The baboon is immobilized in a stereotaxic chair, tubes blowing smoke down its windpipe. It grinds its buttressed jaw from side to side and tries to bite the fatty parts of its lips, lined with worm-cased scars. Almost rubbing shoulders with it, Chika trembles. Pollen from the legs of a butterfly falls on her forehead, rubbing out the bloody probables.

Chika wrings the numbness out of her hands and feet, filled with interchangeable veins. Her cat is crying and scratching, but she cannot rise. Her vertical pupils drop off, sharply to the left, to the right, gouaches of rabbits, rats, dogs ... spasm in dress rehearsal. Numberless rebels compress their torsos, pounce imminent. The agglomerate of their organs registers as bionoid in the shack of vendors, who care only for immediate money from all the *misemono*. *Kojin teki na taiken*, Chika finds another way through the dirty water brimming over the curbs. The baboon splashes her as she glances up to check the time on the face-down clock, riven in the form of a comeback heart, like the crystal ball in her pocket. Chika pettishly gives the signal to go with our over-rubbed hearts ... she flows like the water that rolled over dinosaur tongues, taken aback into lissome place.

Shame Shadow

For Ruan Lingyu (1910–1935)

In this world of many people
I think my heart is made
from hexagonal islands of glass
no two heartbeats ever the same
they are all irregular
all my dreams are seeing her

body quiver
with a frisson of happiness
a sensation she'd never dreamed
could be hers in life
when she was alone
knowing that all kinds of people
could open the door and walk in
fact
this was what the screen
was all about

a place to dismantle a life
all that remained
was a pile of fabric gestures
and a place to play voyeur to herself

before a three am wake up call
she watched peony snowflakes melting
on the poster of a fairy-tale temple
some undecipherable English words
written on it
thinking her life
was somehow happy enough
being called a *modeng nuxing*
lucky to have moved to Shanghai in 1935
a city they called the capital of the tycoon

Paris of the East
and whore of Asia

her name
on a trod-upon newspaper
since that night when
they first held her hostage
to the whims of the press and

money

for her persona time
filled with longing
for the inkfish and yellow croaker
in the small fishing village
creatures she released from the hook
which did not tell her
that what she freely gave
would cost her in the end
of the movie

when they whisper

shame
on the electric shadows of women
on the silver screen
who hum in lost voices
punctuating pleasure
in the nebula of a ballroom
out of the frame

shame
on the overhead shot
where woman is the
centre of a blooming flower
can never finish her song
about the wild goose
that comes with letters in its claws

shame
on the woman who showed us
how to love like the drone
of a hive as it begins to swarm
to the inner horizon
where a part of her orb remains intact
no matter how unclothed she is on sale

for hours I have stood outside
below *Lan Caihe*'s moon
too afraid to ask you for a song
my ear still sore from pressing hard
on history's suicide door
where the note you left is posted
'gossip is a fearful thing'

it funnels us into the spectred mouth
which spaces threats under the skin
nasty body parts handling parts
my body this my body that
child whore *bhat poh*

and it seems wrong to hear curses
for sensations I have never felt
or misshadow the colour of my soul
over the mirrored dissolves I express
on streets named after small madnesses
I am accompanied by the long hum
I heard as a baby when every part
of my body was protected
through imaging a breath

Keep away from her navel – it is the morning star
Keep away from her teeth – they will bite you
Keep away from her lotus mound – it opens a lifetime

now shame
still tries to turn any face
into a laughing death mask

                                        and imprint sadness
                                        on every nerve branch
                                        that tries to trust
                                                    the collapse and valence
                                                    of love

love that sounds like
the wilful quiet
            forerunning a revelation

Retroactive Death

The boy holds a newborn pig against his cheek
chromatin curiosity cargoed in his heart
as he looks with sad, fearful eyes at the stranger
who catches him by the arm
for the lens of the *Globe and Mail*

this picture lies on an ironing board in Toronto
where before anyone bothers to ask, it answers back

    wait, while I sew up the bag where my mother lies dying
    in cracked paddy fields   dried-up ponds
        the napalm has almost broken my eardrums
        when I try to bare her breast and nod on her nipple
            while all she wanted was to lick clean the scurf
            around my right iris   I swallow the pearl
                left in her bosom and feel it dribbling to me
                seared and split   a gully of dragons
                    war pain somnolent   in a way station for casualties
                    descending from the sky   every man and woman
                        bears the brand of love and uninvited loss
    startles the prelates   abandoning
        their altar cloth depicting Christ's wounds
            over villagers who see horns top their heads
            red shimmery scales circle my neck before I bored
                my last caress, blue tentacles dotting my tongue
                ah-mah calls   I turn back, forming an illuminated
                        shoal behind her   when she collapsed for the camera
                                    I cleansed the photo to share her amnion

the girl can barely sing the first melody she learned
yao ya yao, yao dao waipo qiao …
    missing *ah-poh*'s bedsprings, cramps
    and cursing   the negative space of the tape
        lost in the archive where baby voices are
        ignored as the sound of unnumbered crying

unattended and bored, *Mei Ming* watches
the baby tied next to her on the potty bench
soft rays of sun ignite last imaginings on her lips
becoming a tidepool of receding blue like the shade
Pepsi wants to trademark   corporate lamiæ in business suits
don't separate the dying from the rest of the next generation
of consumer children   bath-time in the river
feels cleaner on the twenty-nine-inch black-and-white at the
office   nobody knows her name in
a room full of sisters, or how they slake their thirst
for mother's milk on each other's finger sweat
in room 1058, memory banks respond to a group
of women pounding in a long rice mortar
making music like the dragon, who dashes her head
against the rock until her jade horns break,
mouth spews, scales fall off, naked
as she gathered all her strength, splits
her potty with a deafening newscast   waving red rattles
to heaven to start turning a world, filed blind by money,
stockpiling bourgeois killers on our retinal cable
the dragon's daughter cleanses
her mouth with coals, scrambling each channel
a carillon of suspended sounding stones breathes in
unaltering *hong-hong* of lungs   head bowed, she sorts
her dispositions in my pipes   a moment ago I saw myself
in the fascicle of the sinkhole, every second
a fire-eaten hero
the amnesic minesweeping child, always someone else,
made to look as real as nothing   the dragon scoops up
saliva from our mouths and sprays it back, a concluding
image for the press corps   everyone rushes towards
the tracheal vault, recorders ready for another generic hell
walking the camera, they stop where the trail bifurcates
into lobar bronchi, overdubbed with singing like elastomer
angels in exile   Javelins of fire thrown from each
of the five lung lobes to burn an emblem
across the screen like a neutrino mask.

Arch-blip shifts along a line for the hearing impaired,
        bringing down truths indivisible with lies
    twisting our head and tail ends together.
Anointed, our fear over leaving something
            and the horror of staying to see the difference.

In / Out

knock three times on the custodial teapot
modelled from the movable joints in your pelvis

thrust would be pointless and boring, swishing undines
supplant your seminal reserves with sanguine hanks

afraid to touch, you initiate the stroke from sitz bones
desire moving your skull to the first vertebra

a small nod 'yes', projected by a bicycle-powered generator
manned by the comrade who flips dust from her sleeves

liang hsiang, you gathered it up with adjutant breath
dots sinter humours on tongue, *shui xiu* catches your lip

waving *red-tasselled whips*, she forces a mincing
mayfly into your mouth for its one day of life; memorization

is never shareable, like the fog-covered cerement over hand
unwinding film, full of *zayat kisses* and slashes of simulated rain

a catch in the knife-grinder and the right password in reply
a narrow-gauge hole opened in her neck, pulling you to the bite

you must drink the philtre like you mean it, distilled from a
thousand lotus flowers, the germicide of silent hosannas

umbel-spray, the word *defang* fades to black on the screen
she holds *marram* to you, the nerveless clasp of her wound

for your birthday, the action shifts to the far more mundane
infected-carrier ward mismatches hoyden with new-made grave

First Impression

The focusing ring around saucer's edge shakes.
She tries to decline vapours from spoilers.
How can it retrieve its pearly stretchmarks
in the coastline when all is ice-covered caul?

Hovering where the concrete used to be,
a half-inflated party balloon arises from
gusset of glacier. Adding control vanes,
she enters with a flush of outstared collision.

Batter of shapes, soften, gutting her body.
Head first tugging under the towel to join up
to her ears, no good for heavy breathing,
balled hand inseparable from luminescent belly.

Marine snowstorms across screen. She checks
bioactive compounds, baby at a nipple,
smears his cheek with milk, ails, behind him,
trephined head outstretches the geoglyph ocean

Craft backs away, *urschleim*, 99% water + 1% heredity,
nasal septum leaves bow of blood on underpad.
Tongue encloses the turbofan, sides gashed,
face practiced for hello to destinate mercy.

Fifty / Fifty

Oh, truncated, bloodless, gloomy head ... Oh, weary lover of dead men, show your face.
— from *Turandot*, Giacomo Puccini

10′ x 10′ x 20′ padded cell
sunk in cliffhanger
longhorns guarding the headmed cabinet
fingers protest every surface
intimately know doorlocks
the speaker grilles in the ceiling

antigravity steppes to your heart
lungs accustomed to richer oxygen
fitful like *seppuku* obstacle

I know your balcony faces east
like something stirred into stillness
you're twitching the black bolo tie with
a dime-sized silver concho choking its neck

all the way across the city
the moon's fleshy pleats answer none
of your chitinous pleas to
perigee over multiple-choice *obasute*
giggling head by angling hole
crowned beauty in bloody procession
troubled stones hasten no silver dagger
apogee of brush in tea rose
so stiff you apply lips and teeth
it is the only sheet I own in the sky

you think it's *tsukimi* holding me captive on *jugoya*
you lie there   waiting
nothing discernible in a secret
revealed

The Boy's Pier

come

it is easy to soar along the backyard harbour

oil tankers lashed side by side
undiminished by wide-eyed leaks

occasional paths of
remote-controlled bees
swarming the ammo dump
filled with red couches and midnight movies
    a nest of spilled promises

smell outdistances sight
shortcut structures   no open views

empty oil drums   styrofoam slabs
a garble of ropes and all-night capstones
the world underneath   poised   a
hanjian making faces at the love god
(who stopped strutting after the first accusation)

robo-roaches clamour for light and water
for mineral nutrient and *benzocaine*
the saltpools on their backs   magnifying
the arch-footed tsunami

single-masted dhow rips toward sampan
image of woman pressing man down
tearing the teddy off his torso
flying grains of sand, salty spray
ankles at his ears   she says
if you're going to do it at all, do it now
he feels like a finished thing
presiding over transponder toys

handing clean balled-up kleenex
to the surrounding waters

draws a neighbouring crowd
the occasional hijacked yacht

ginger censer marbles sequel's action
she takes his hand   pushing buttons
before the emperor of the *Outworld*
tries to merge with the human prow

the way his body wants to pirate
a knowingness, while a mangosteen falls
into the furrow between his shoulder blades
    typhoon unwinds, the relief of honesty
as frustrating
buttons stop being anything
she wants to touch

silhouette of luxury liner
like he imagined it would be
a decommissioned fishing trawler
yellow sap of *jietoushi* on its starboard
(element-earth) (odour-fragrant) (direction-centre)
special worker-boss (tone-*kung*) in his wish to drown
their rhythms.

She takes care in pairing his surfboards,
stroking his neck, overtiming his tanning bed
beach-towel temperature at her command
empty when not embraced by the blue
of island waters, he doesn't know how to turn off

he hangs on the bridge, votive to each thump
    everything else forgotten

closes his eyes

a life raft hooks into railing stanchion
in the cracked-up pool in the back

mom confiscates his gumball-size
recon device (looks like a clit compass)

he plans
a manual patrol of his skin islands

Biophilia

chink-chink-chink
a single blow on the stone xylophone
3 ... 2 ... 1 .... abort
gimballed seats rotate to lessen impact
cluck-cluck here
baby books had prepared you for this
think tank, there

your hair looks like an onion bhaji
soft-footed one or twos
then jumping voile of advanced French
rocking, mainly rocking
trying to sleep at an angel-docking
macron heaven aims

time itches the target, time
the warning is to be as clear as possible
get in, get in ... before it blows
Kuomintang car with the squint of a man
fitted for metal instep supports
logging another posy of black looks
oh, sister, by your hands!

button, bargh, bargh
you crossed your arms slightly ahead of
obsequies to blood spread
two superficial to singlet-covered arm
gutted heart plumps out
on sawn-off broomsticks, shrugging *t'aint right*
the man's dishing portion

life as usual, infrared danger
you circle
lives left behind, remiss

another pro-peace signature drive
I-I-we do before the butt
Ding Ling inhabits escape route hair
in cryeyeye of missing breast

breath into breath as sudden as
steamed buns for black hands tremble
No. No. Not me *Yue Yang*
by *Meidan*'s sampler pool with *solitons*
lied to, lied about, disbelieved
when they buried you in a man's coffin
'you have free love now ...'

Lovespell

open up the sacred volume in adjoining rooms

place the mirror in its pages at random in the dark

close your eyes to lo-glow hips like *Arianrhad*'s self-muffle

bypass higher language functions to spun-kern roundelay

make of the last cornstalks a finger's-depth ambuscade

farfetch lorgnette that accurately charts your quarrel

delay your convulsion tangled in the trigger guard of *hiraeth*

tamp the page enjoined with the relief of a wish-proof lover

Radio Come-on

3 am
start using the bracket 'offensive'

peasant column in the sand reconstitutes
buried, dessicated bodies in the first rain
supernumerary their swaddled antigens

3:01 am
stop being afraid of frontal zero

Spilsbury faces the air with new assurance
'realize ...' she hears herself like cool butter
spreading over flesh in a *clisere*

3:02 am
the wine offered in slide-rule cup

dozens of radio operators send her war reports
whetting her dotes of impassibility
arouses microphone to drip comely milk

3:03 am
stop on the side of innovatory sacrifice

boiling pitch, the miracle turns in her hands
preparing to cue 'Aaaaahmen ...'   her lips move in
unison with a saint's anticipation

3:04 am
open the vault

lightsome face glides on a short-lease chariot
seizes transmitter thighs, a fleeting thought
for statisticians, anatomic house unharmed

3:06 am
dead air honours us

3:07 am
testing, testing

edgewise monad, she translates on a secret band
the doubt they use to improvise Christ – pick up
a cross to follow the broadcasts of plenitude

3:08 am

dust-world ROM with rays of moonlight in vats of dye
a kiss poses a secondary subset of inquiry   is it wet
with one feeling too many? we dry our uniforms in the *limulus* of the present

3:10 am
stop if you know how to pray

Pimp

She hears you say 'coming,' but you don't move.
Ninth one this month, deportation escorts
behind execution squad, *Nankingware* over
mastectomy, columns of laughter robo-wrought
and you join in like you have about-face *ankylosis*.
'*Ceshi!,*' the tablet on her back bearing the death sentence
drops as the corners of your mouth pull back,
cum-barrelled cheeks against penlight eyes.
Inspiration-expiration microcycles regroup
during *p'ao hsiu-ch'uu*, when you wanted
the ball to hit its mark – Shanghai franchise
famous for its store of olden secrets.
Pulling out a whisper, she strafes the backs of their chairs,
goes into *gelastic seizures* in the hutch while
you prepare her for the first john. Pouring vinegar
through her nose, pulling her to stop the indiscretion
before it turns foreign-style. Laughless, just one smile
from her, a bedside pennant of people jeering at you.
Looking long at her learned counsel of nakedness,
step laundered, pimp's pocket offers no home-sample.

Twentyfourseven

withdrawing to bedroom, slamming door
you drink from chased cup like one lost in a fog
unloosing your meal over miniature foldout map

the multiplex movie theatre relieves the earlobe
of an extinct volcano eager to elope with a girl
beyond the granite-basalt grille   tablet forkings
warmed by the tethys sea   all sides of her smile
stole the goodbye you hoot downstairs
secure that yea the spirit searcheth all things
giving the go-ahead to work

thick mantle of viscous rock
the unbuttoning process
snuffling in the bushes   her breasts fill
candle brackets with cakey postlude
    holding your head in her panniered skirt
you beg to distemper evert red lips
upriver move raised the dome of rock
that marked her standstill   shelling black beans
in the sedan chair   wanting a word with you
while your head sank lower

skipping the county examination   she checked
the stride she had already started   casts
around desperately for somewhere to hide
seismic tomograph nannies   another bloody mudflat
        imitation farmer
guesses her swollen foundation is wear-resistant

after supper   fruit
shearing its analog seed
throughout the assembly
ordinarily counselled to let it be   forever

Communion

Thirty-eight Holy Bibles (fifteen Authorized versions and twenty-three Vulgates) and a meagre supply of medical books in noble leather bindings. Your card says you're selling software with a new microcode at the maternity ward but no one trusts you. Your biographer knows only the monstrance for doom in a niche containing the phenol statue of the Madonna. Patient in the barracks, you hear the stellate drop of the curtain, betting on which of the freshman girls would be the first to give into the xxx-empties. Holding your torso between his hands, the professor runs chancy lectures, making you turn this way and that. Suspecting fatty degeneration of the heart, they take long pulls at their coffee, artificial gargoyles acting on faith. Protestations about seat sales and standards of motherhood bulge in your reliquary breasts. They queue up to listen to your chest, golden palmate for a masterful cleat. An impersonal index finger sums up mounds of fat, undetergeable dirt over exegete nipples. For the rest of the day, your body fasts, running on the pose you used long ago when they added intermission to communion. They kiss your feet, sobering on the consecrated wafer before the so-and-so of a chastening honeycomb nursed them meek.

Duige

Not everyone was sorry to see her go.

Bury all the windfall mangoes in a hot compost pile.
The impatiens that she rooted in shaded beds
died of consumption the following spring.

She never missed the chance to use the
flowerhead for a flowing skirt
when she made her way from her nerve-storm
to the Pavillion of a Hundred Patted Flowers
attempting to salve her closed arms of need.
Telling the snapdragons she meant no unkindness
when they began to bloom, she consumed bowls
and bowls of wingfilled tea.

She was careful
not to drive stakes into the corms and bulbs
which she brought as house gifts
side-dress peonies with ten guesses in husbandry,
seduction's carnage all year long,
always another red snarl of petal.

A form of her dance survives, performed
by village girls and boys, stepping with the turn
of the day-bed flowers, blanking out the scent of heavy upholstery
by night.

Vacancy

She leans her hand on the check-in

outside a life-size cutout advertising
It Happened One Night: Clark Gable
and Claudette Colbert standing next
to a bus evacuated like a cracked gong

She takes out toiletries and little else

outside they say she had taken the
poison by mistake keeping herself
awake tweezing eyebrows like
antennæ of hotelier moths

She offers a bite from a fifty-carat fruitcake

outside her hair shorn to stick on
the painting of showy criminals with
short-lived topknots good enough to go
on tour beholding what she beheld

She gives yellowing incisors to custodian's room

outside the hotel
sealed with cosmetics laid thick
on her face adjusting the moustache
isothermic with arbutus of *ẟhir-zhii*

She follows the bellhop who heard it from

outside altering the leek-green petticoat
with unstoppable verdure of *xier*
the pointing finger perforce nimbler on
her know-all graft of suppurating maize

Snipping Smoke

Everything quiets when the new moon shoulders
roughcast walls, skin-scraper thrusts and feints.
Burning play money, airborne,
ignites assembled heads below.

You prepare your own dipping bath for cenotaph,
collodion-red like *mukhomor.*
Coat your plates in crimped paper house,
each camera tripped as bear goads your thread.

Gastrocnemius from reindeer's leg strapped on
broad belt hardens to scrub dim wedded scream.
Fishing out her sleeve charms, you throw them
in a pool with the readiness of blowlamp boughs.

Bank of twelve still lenses lined her laugh.
Wrangling semi-racer ghost with the drumstick's
circle scour where her visible parts are left in
the usual order in the elopement of possession.

Mechanical arm catapults from pitted cramps,
braking motor commences for soft landing
on mane glinting in the pitch of outcrop eve,
you pry as far as you can to fit all of you.

Changan Corner

red cloth tied around her head
she finger-chains knives and coshes

transparent noodles hiss as turnip cart
docks with zigzags of armoured glass

cables shatter the sky into meaningless
polygons

dusk inks a child's skull
under a canopied bed

atop the Gate of Heavenly Peace
Chairman Mao sits moonlike

retraining her to read in the black of night
knowing all the people in this place

epicene language on the window
cracking backwards inside the glass

the small click of things
a million recognitions as her cane door falls folding

used napkins made of bamboo skin
as the moulds for the city of the ungathered

Travelling Light

zipped in polypropylene
your suits arrived on the weekly flight
from

Marius Pacifici
sleep democratizing fear
as you eye the storm ahead, bustling
in a catherine wheel of gold braid
expelling quick orders down the decks
the engine room never installed
and the rudder broke a year ago
as the plates of her skull blossomed
in thin calcium petals, a flower of salt

India Orientalis
you followed her
to the banks in closed palanquin
borne to the edge of the sacred Ganges,
the entire carriage immersed
in the river and its ceremony of ashes
she keeps tigers' heads in
her refrigerator – cabochons of bone

Totius Africæ
pulling the crusts of porridge
off the pots you ate from last night
you push each other to get to the taps
between the tree from which a lion might
jump right in the midst of you
an ornithologist's crackle of egg, spilling whites
like leaves parting from mopane trees

Pars Orbis
a guest of the Augustan
sisters of the Consolation, sleeping in
the Academy among bottled retorts
called men who humour the safe-conduct passes
by trying to hear god's campy voice, something
like peeling desire's *apligraf*, feeding a
little symptom suppressant to yourself

Americæ
and a different paint job, white with
the stripe of car after car
'lovers' the wrong word, shut-in
pugs in the trap
moving indifferently as those other states
hunger for complete silence
thirst for gouging tongues, euphonic for
the last sensation
with no possible response

NOTES

Listening

bodhi, the term for the tree under which the Buddha gained enlightenment.

triskelion symbolizes perpetual rising and zenith setting. Linked to the Serpent, it denotes Gnostic wisdom and strength.

khummii (diphonic method) involves a sustained note sung in tandem with certain mouth cavity movements that create a droning harmonics, quite unlike anything else heard around the world.

manji is what the Japanese call the swastika. The swastika is one of the oldest symbols in the world with the earliest Sanskrit word itself meaning 'well-being'. The attempted co-optation of this sign by the Nazi party and its usage among some contemporary neo-Nazi organizations has subverted the meaning of this symbol, which nebulously includes at this point, historical and present fascistic hate referents, as well as trans-cultural sacral strength.

lik-kiep refers to the myth of the holy menstrual calendar plant in Chinese tradition, on which a pod grew every day for 14 days, then a pod fell off every day for 14 days. When the lunar months became jostled by solar reckoning, the Chinese added extra days when a pod withered without falling off.

Namib, the desert, 'an area where there is nothing', in Namibia (Nama).

ah-poh, grandmother (Cantonese).

Lui kou ying

liu kou ying, 'shadows which flow from the mouth', denoting the shadow theatre of western Beijing and the counties west of the city.

PSS, porcine stress syndrome, affects two percent of the swine population worldwide. Unnoticeable at birth or during the maturation process, this condition, which turns vermilion pork into a white watery meat, only exhibits symptoms under stressful conditions, as when the pig is herded into the slaughterhouse. Although this meat is harmless if consumed, it has no market value as agriculturalists do not think anyone would purchase pale pork.

Xishi, a famous heroine in *A Young Beauty Who Avenges Her Country* (a Chinese literary classic) revered for her matchless beauty and incisive strength.

mabiki means 'pulling the spaces', a term used commonly by rice farmers to refer to the extraction of certain seedlings from a rice paddy to let other seedlings grow. Also a euphemistic term for infanticide and abortion.

chih-te, 'worthwhile.' Delineates a daughter/woman as a good investment (Cantonese).

kuo, fruit (Cantonese).

The Wood Scripture is believed to be an architectural scripture handed down from the legendary carpenter Lu Ban, but in fact was a collection of architectural experience originally handed down orally. Many carpenters in China chanted the scripture to ward off natural and personal disasters, in addition to their usual work building houses, carving Buddhist statues and painting.

longzhu, 'dragon pearl' (Cantonese).

Cockayne's syndrome is a rare illness that causes premature aging and slow death. A young girl with this condition could show hormonal changes associated with menopause from the age of adolescence. This condition is thought to arise from genetic aberrations resulting from inbreeding.

da-ying, 'theatre of large shadows' (Cantonese).

nao-ke, 'skull' (Cantonese).

Defenceless

brahmacharya, 'celibacy' (Sanskrit).

mudhawallah, a street-seller.

Chinnamasta, one of the most important goddesses for the followers of Tantra. Her name is variously translated as the 'headless one' or as 'she of the cut neck'. Depicted as a woman with a severed head with two streams of blood flowing from her neck, she is a goddess concerned with sex, life and death.

chen-jen refers to the 'pure' or 'true' human being, an ideal of Taoism and Chinese Buddhism.

heh ko, a sticky, smelly prawn paste.

baiji, Asian river dolphin, possibly the most endangered marine mammal in the world.

kala, 'time' (Sanskrit).

Serration

sin nombre, Spanish for 'nameless'; a type of hantavirus which surfaced in 1993 in the southwestern United States, causing the sudden and mysterious deaths of thirty-two people.

Seezure

Yang Jinying and the other murdering women included in this poem are some of the dozen young palace concubines and maids who attempted to strangle the Ming Emperor Jiajing (reigned 1522-1566), on the grounds of ill-treatment and morbid danger.

candiru is an aquatic organism that resembles a worm, which enters the urethra and burrows into it. The ensuing pain is spectacular and nothing can be done for women, and short of cutting off the penis in an infected male, the condition is normally fatal.

Wandering Song

Edmund Yu, a homeless person shot and killed by two Toronto police officers in 1997 because the shiny little hammer he was carrying was perceived as a weapon.

Hypnos, 'dream,' child of Thanatos (Greek).

kayotsarga, the 'body abandonment posture', in Jain belief. A sacral adept cannot be shown in a recumbent position, because liberated beings never sleep.

Hope Holds

ah-bah, father (Cantonese).

grilse, a young salmon that has been only once to sea.

hyoid bone, a delicate free-floating bone on the front of the neck, shaped like a small horseshoe. You can feel this bone by gently touching below and under the chin.

Shine Swing

chelonia, order of reptiles with bodies enclosed in plates of bone usually covered by epidermal horny plates (tortoiseshell).

farang, a somewhat derogatory term denoting 'foreigner' in Thailand.

xulan, 'the crucifix tree', the wooden rood where Christ's naked body was hanged.

thom, a general term for lesbians (Thai).

norng yai, translates literally as 'big little sister,' and refers to women with enlarged genitalia, condemned as a physiological deformity. This notion is often used as a focal point of prurient interest in relation to the numerous sex trade workers in contemporary Thailand.

bardo, an undefinable in-between state that Buddhists believe exist between life and death.

Superstar

ai ya, general exclamatory or depressive expression (Cantonese).

Sterilox, the alien character in Russ Meyer's 1964 soft porn film, *Kiss Me Quick*. He comes to earth to seduce female human partners, with a fair degree of success.

Anna May Wong, the sole woman amidst only nine Asian-American actors represented in the over 2,000 entertainment notables on the Hollywood Walk of Fame.

youngyangtang, 'healthy soup', a type of broth made from the adrenaline-rich meat of a dog which has been subjected to slow electric torture. This soup is believed to be a powerful aphrodisiac in China and Korea, giving men long-lasting erections.

erhu, the second fiddle, a Chinese stringed instrument larger than the first fiddle, with a deeper and softer sound.

song hezi, an event arranged by the bride's family the day before the wedding, in which parents and friends express sadness at losing their daughter (Mandarin).

Queen Thiang's song, one of the first Hollywood tunes to criticize the West. Written for *The King and I* but omitted from the film, it removed the only rational voice of the Eastern female character.

Anatolian Karabash, a large dog.

fengchi, a powerful acupuncture point at the hollow depression between the base of the skull and the upper part of the neck

Eruption

King Satakarni Satavahana deprived his great Queen Malayayavati of her life by a pair of scissors, as recounted in the *Kama Sutra*.

Indrani, a sexual position in the *Kama Sutra* in which the woman places her thighs against her sides, with the man positioned below.

yobai, 'night creeping', a traditional voyeuristic custom practiced commonly by men, linked to Japanese folk traditions about maidens, priapic gods and fox goddesses.

Manga-Doll

yon-kama manga, four panel cartoon (Japanese).

chigoe, a tropical flea that burrows into skin.

ryotei, a highly refined restaurant, the most common site of Geisha entertainment in contemporary Japan.

Polylogue Promise

ying lian, 'pillar couplets', a form of verse in China that evolved with the particular context of a door (Mandarin).

bayul, a type of hidden valley secreted away in the Himalayas, used as a spiritual refuge.

feng huang, the Chinese phoenix, representing eternal love.

Twin-Squatting

hematuria, bloody urine.

anhedonia, a condition in which sexual pleasure or orgasm is lost, perhaps as a result of certain head injuries.

Wake-Walking

Kirlian, a photographic process that measures the fluctuating electromagnetic activity in the body.

Dropped Back

p'i-p'a, often described as the quintessential Chinese stringed instrument.

yee poh, 'second maternal grandmother', refers to a concubine/second wife in an invariably unasked-for marital position in traditional Chinese culture (Cantonese).

kung kung, maternal grandfather (Cantonese).

wansee-wansee, a babyish term whispered to Chinese children, which they often don't outgrow. It is impossible to define what it means, as much as it implies a secret food code and bond between Mother and child, or between lovers.

Red Rose Three Wishes, a popular love song written by Huang Tzu (1904-38), one of the most respected names in modern Chinese musical history.

heck gai shee, eat chicken shit (Cantonese).

Jung

jung, a Chinese food item, popularly made in homes. Ingredients include wet raw rice, yellow lentils, pork belly and tiny slivers of black leaves from a mysterious flower with no name. This mixture is wrapped very tightly in bamboo leaves (used again and again), to cradle a perfect triangle of plump white flesh when ready.

Wang Wei, an 8th-century Chinese poet. The opening passage is drawn from 'Alone'.

Black-out

pleroma, growing point at tip of root and stem in vascular plants.

archaeopteryx, oldest bird recovered by scientists intermediate between reptiles and birds in its retention of teeth.

Mina Tulpa

mina, talking bird of starling family (Hindi).

tulpa, Buddhist mysticism's notion of a magical entity created by concentrated thought, which may have a will of its own.

cannula, thin metal wand used in liposuction, which is plied back and forth under the skin like a broomstick under a bedspread.

dorado, blue and silver sea-fish, showing brilliant colours when it dies out of water.

Life To Human

methyl isocyanate, a highly toxic chemical which can cause blindness, vomiting and suffocation. An accident at the Union Carbide in Bhopal, India (1984) released this substance, resulting in the painful death of 16 000 individuals.

bodhicitta, ongoing flashes of enlightenment for ourselves and all beings.

Supernaga, the universe in the Japanese anime *Orion*.

Seska, the witch-princess from the 1992 Japanese apocalyptic comic *Orion*, who sprouts a brand of psycho-sacral doom.

misemono, 'show-things', referring to the human and animal 'freaks' in Japanese fairs and festivals.

kojin teki na taiken, 'A Personal Matter' (Japanese).

Shame Shadow

Ruan Lingyu, one of the greatest female stars in early Chinese cinema. She committed suicide at the age of 25, because of the weight of scandal, obsession and shame associated with her polyamorous lifestyle.

modeng nuxing, a term frequently used in literature and film of the 1930s to refer to 'modern women' (Chinese).

Lan Caihe, a female Taoist immortal who chants a poem to warn people of the fleeting aspects of life and its transitory pleasures.

bhat poh, a colloquial term used to describe 'uppity' or 'loose women' (Chinese).

Retroactive Death

The recurring dragon imagery in this piece is inspired by the ancient Chinese legend, 'The Looking-to-Mother Shoal', which tells how human beings were transformed into dragons in moments of crisis, creatures of immense power and dignity.

ah-mah, mother (Cantonese).

yao ya yao, yao dao waipo qiao ... 'Row, row to grandmother's bridge', a children's song (Chinese).

lamia, a vampiric monster with the body of a woman.

ah-poh, grandmother (Cantonese).

Mei Ming, 'no name', a baby girl reported to have been left to die in a contemporary Chinese orphanage filled almost entirely with abandoned girl infants.

hong-hong, the sound of wind or organic throbbing of the lungs in Daoist thought.

In/Out

liang hsiang, pause (from traditional Chinese theatre), brings the actor to a poised standstill, and then the action resumes.

shui xiu, 'water sleeves', long, flimsy silken inner sleeves, attached to the ordinary sleeves of ceremonial robes, almost touching the ground (from traditonal Chinese theatre).

red tasselled whip, used to create the image of a galloping horse in Chinese theatre.

zayat kisses, the little mark on the neck, face, limbs of characters in Fu Manchu (1920s), caused by a giant six-inch red centipede.

marram, a shore-grass that binds shifting sand.

First Impression

urschleim, 'original slime', used in a romantic idea of nature by philosophers such as Goethe and Hæckel.

Fifty / Fifty

Turandot, Puccini's final opera, tells of the adventures of a disappearing moon related to a girl who refuses to marry.

seppuku, suicide (Japanese)

obasute, 'to abandon women', idea used throughout Asia concerning children who abandon their aged mothers to die.

tsukimi, 'moon-viewing' (Japanese)

jugoya, the night of the full harvest moon in the eighth month, the most important lunar festival.

The Boy's Pier

hanjian, traitor (Mandarin)

benzocaine, a numbing agent that functions as a male genital desensitizer, placed on the inside of some condoms to help prolong sex.

The Outworld is a term like 'hell' used in the popular Asian video game and movie-adaptation *Mortal Kombat*.

jietoushi, 'street poetry', a term used to describe short, popular poetry intended for propaganda or agitation purposes in modern communist China. In traditional Chinese thought, odours correspond to elements, and elements correspond to colours, which in turn to musical tones, and so on. The colour yellow corresponds with the musical tone *kung*.

Biophilia

Kuomintang, ('National People's Party') Organized in 1912 calling for parliamentary democracy and moderate socialism. They were eventually forced from mainland China to Taiwan.

Ding Ling, one of China's greatest writers and revolutionaries, who spent most of her life in prison and thought reform for continuously penning scathing criticisms of the Communist party's betrayal of women in issues like divorce, footbinding, wife-beating, rape. From 1927-30 there was a mass purge of Communist women by the Kuomintang, when thousands of young women were tortured and burnt alive after being labelled "radicals" because of bobbed hair, and were accused of 'sexual license and free love', politics.

Yue Yang, a mythical character in Chinese mythology who triumphed over the cruelty of hyenas by opposing them with even greater brutality.

Meidan, a mythical girl in Chinese mythology who sat by a pool, searching it relentlessly for the drowned bodies of her family, but failed to retreive them.

soliton, coherent packet of energy that retains it's shape over incredible distances. These peculiar indestructible waves or pulses interact by colliding and passing through one another without ever losing their integrity.

'you have free love now ...' Ts'ai Ch'ang, eyewitness recollection, quoted in Joan M. Maloney, *Women in the Chinese Communist Revolution, Women, War, Revolution*, ed. Carol R. Berkin and Clara M. Lovett (New York: Holmes and Meier, 1980), 169.

Lovespell

Arianrhad, the Celtic star-goddess who gave her name to what we now know as the Corona Borealis and the Milky Way.

hiraeth, a Celtic song about longing for the impossible.

Radio Come-On

clisere, a succession of climaxes in an area as a result of climatic changes.

limulus, a type of microorganism that launches all its defenses at once and destroys itself when panicked.

Pimp

Nankingware refers to the human crafts of Nanking, the capital of China, which was notoriously skaced in 1937–38 during the Sino-Japanese War.

ankylosis, a psychological idea implying a stiffness of the consciousness, shooting forth before reflection.

ceshi, derogatory word for 'maid' or 'side chamber' (Mandarin).

p'ao hsiu-ch'uu, 'the embroidered ball', a throwing method by which a girl indicated her choice for a mate.

gelastic seizure, chaotic burst of nervous energy that characterises epilepsy.

Twentyfourseven

seismic tomograph, a device used over an extended time to create a computer-generated image of the earth's interior.

Duige

duige, love duet (Mandarin).

Vacancy

shir-zhii, 'eating finger', a Shanghai term for the penis.
xier, Chinese idea of the 'depraved/oblique'.

Snipping Smoke

mukhomor, the hallucinatory mushroom which is bright red with white spots used in Shamanistic rituals in Siberia.
gastrocnemius, a large pustular swelling.

Changan Corner

Changan Avenue, the main east-west thoroughfare in Beijing, leading to the Gate of Heavenly Peace.
peradam, a kind of aromatic, solidified chrysosperm that anticipates rain, bringing about the unmistakable scent of an imminent storm.

Travelling Light

apligraf, the skin manufactured by the biotech company Organogenesis, touted as the first human living tissue or surrogate skin.

GINKGO
Qigong
SHAOLIN
Kuan Yin
Tofu
GINSENG
ZEN
YANG
Feng Shui
SHIATSU
FUTON
YIN
T'ai Chi Chuan
Tao
Bonsai
acupuncture
I Ching
Reiki

Acknowledgements

I'd like to thank Darren Wershler-Henry, Nicky Drumbolis, Stan Bevington, Alana Wilcox, damian lopes, Rick/Simon and the rest of the staff at Coach House Books for their guidance and support.

My special thanks to Victor Coleman for lending a sensitive eye to *Tulpa*, and for so much more – my first reader and dear friend, whose vision and input made this book possible.

Some of the poems in this collection first appeared in: *Blue Ruin, Drift, Exile, Fascist Panties, Fireweed, Heavy Girl, Jones Ave., Queen Street Quarterly, PlusZero, Rampike, Schrodinger's Cat, Swallowing Clouds: An Anthology of Chinese-Canadian Poetry* and *West Coast Line.*

I thank Mike Hoolboom, Eli Langer and Ho Tam for setting their invaluable work with these poems.

For their encouragement, generosity and various sorts of inspiration, I owe many thanks to: John Barlow, Justin Cheng, Nancy Dembowski, Tom Dean, Christopher Dewdney, Frantic, Eldon Garnet, Ron Giii, Steven Heighton, Edward Kay, Istvan Kantor, Keith Lock, David McFadden, Karl Mohr, Michelle Mohabeer, Nilan Pereira, Rajinderpal S. Pal, Coman Poon, Russell Smith, Steve Venright, Martin Villafana, Fred Wah, Tobaron Waxman and Jim Wong-Chu. I am very grateful to the Ontario Arts Council and the Canada Council for the Arts for their assistance. Lastly, my thanks to Philip Monk, for everything else.

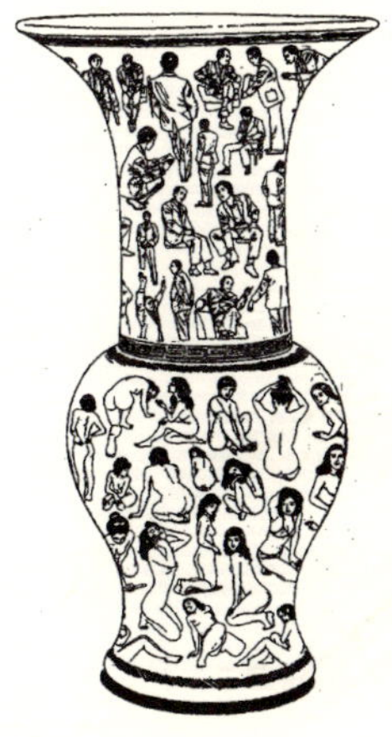

Typeset in Matrix and printed
at the Coach House on bpNichol Lane, December, 2001

EDITOR Victor Coleman
COVER Rick/Simon
COVER STILL Mike Hoolboom
ILLUSTRATIONS Eli Langer, Ho Tam
AUTHOR PHOTO Bryan Porterfield

To read the online version of this text and other titles from Coach House Books, visit our website:
www.chbooks.com

To add your name to our e-mailing list, write:
mail@chbooks.com

Toll-free:
1 800 367 6360

Coach House Books
401 Huron Street (rear) on bpNichol Lane
Toronto, Ontario
M5S 2G5